MW00814947

CRIMEBUSTING and DETECTION

HÉLÈNE BOUDREAU

Crabtree Publishing Company

www.crabtreebooks.com

Crabtree Publishing Company
www.crabtreebooks.com

Author: Hélène Boudreau
Project editor: Tom Jackson
Designer: Lynne Lennon
Picture researcher: Sophie Mortimer
Indexer: Kay Ollerenshaw
Managing editor: Miranda Smith
Art director: Jeni Child
Design manager: David Poole
Editorial director: Lindsey Lowe
Children's publisher: Anne O'Daly
Editor: Michael Hodge
Proofreaders: Adrianna Morganelli, Crystal Sikkens
Project coordinator: Robert Walker
Production coordinator: Katherine Berti
Font management: Mike Golka
Prepress technician: Katherine Berti

This edition published in 2009 by
Crabtree Publishing Company.

The Brown Reference Group plc,
First Floor, 9–17 St. Albans Place,
London, N1 0NX
www.brownreference.com

Copyright © 2009 The Brown Reference Group plc

Photographs

Corbis: Bettmann: p. 26 (bottom); Andrew Brookes: p. 12–13, 18 (bottom); Anna Clopet: p. 13 (center right), 16 (top); Kim Kullish: p. 28–29; Thierry Orban/Sygma: p. 16 (bottom); Andy Toensing/Sygma: p. 15 (bottom)
Rex Features: Denis Closon: p. 11 (bottom), 20 (top); Roger-Viollet: p. 9 (bottom)
Science Photo Library: John Clegg: p. 23 (bottom); Mauro Fermariello: p. 10 (bottom right), 19 (bottom), 21 (bottom), 25 (top), 27; Peter Menzel p. 22–23 (top); Philippe Psaila: p. 5 (bottom right), 7 (center right), 10–11 (top), 17 (top); Tek Image: cover
Shutterstock: Simone Conti: p. 20 (bottom right); Jack Dagley Photography: p. 6 (bottom left), 8; Sean Gladwell: 25 (bottom); Just/ASC: p. 6 (top); Vadim Kozlovsky: p. 13 (bottom left); Thomas Mounsey: p. 23 (bottom left); Pakhnyushcha: p. 24–25; Pertusinas: p. 18–19; Rae: p. 12 (bottom left), 15 (top right); Loren Rogers: p. 4–5; Scott Rothstein: p. 9 (top); Stavchansky: p. 17 (bottom right); stock: p. 24 (bottom); Leah-Anne Thompson: p. 21 (top); Tara Urbach: p. 6–7
Topfoto: David R. Frazier/Image Works: p. 14; Phil Penman: p. 28 (bottom)

Illustration
Mark Walker: p. 26

Every effort has been made to trace the owners of copyrighted material.

Library and Archives Canada Cataloguing in Publication

Boudreau, Hélène, 1969-
Crimebusting and detection / Hélène Boudreau.

(Science solves it)
Includes index.
ISBN 978-0-7787-4167-1 (bound).–ISBN 978-0-7787-4174-9 (pbk.)

1. Forensic sciences–Juvenile literature. 2. Criminal investigation–Juvenile literature. I. Title. II. Series: Science solves it (St. Catharines, Ont.)

HV8073.8.B67 2008   j363.25   C2008-903270-5

Library of Congress Cataloging-in-Publication Data

Boudreau, Hélène.
Crimebusting and detection / Hélène Boudreau.
p. cm. – (Science solves it)
Includes index.
ISBN-13: 978-0-7787-4174-9 (pbk. : alk. paper)
ISBN-10: 0-7787-4174-5 (pbk. : alk. paper)
ISBN-13: 978-0-7787-4167-1 (reinforced library binding : alk. paper)
ISBN-10: 0-7787-4167-2 (reinforced library binding : alk. paper)
1. Criminal investigation–Juvenile literature. 2. Crime scene searches–Juvenile literature. 3. Forensic sciences–Juvenile literature. I. Title. II. Series.

HV8073.8.B68 2009
363.25–dc22

2008021970

Printed in the U.S.A./102017/HF20170912

Crabtree Publishing Company

www.crabtreebooks.com   1-800-387-7650

Published in Canada
Crabtree Publishing
616 Welland Ave.
St. Catharines, ON
L2M 5V6

Published in the United States
Crabtree Publishing
PMB 59051
350 Fifth Ave., 59th FLoor
New York, NY 10118

CONTENTS

Forensic scientists help police solve crimes. They gather **evidence**, conduct tests, and run **experiments** to explain how crimes happened and to help identify criminals.

There are a lot of clues at a crime scene. A forensic scientist's job is to figure out the truth behind clues. Many of the subjects you study in school—biology, physics, chemistry, and computer science—help forensic scientists catch criminals and set innocent people free. These subjects can also be used to find missing persons or identify the victims of accidents.

While the detectives interview witnesses, forensic scientists find other clues to tell the story. After a murder, useful clues include fingerprints, bullet cases, **fibers** from the killer's clothes, and any traces of blood. When there's been a traffic accident, **investigators** measure tire marks and inspect the damage to reconstruct what happened.

A crime scene is sealed off by the police while a team of scientists makes sure it is safe and look for clues.

SITE SAFETY OFFICER

DO NOT CROSS

TEAM EFFORT

Forensic scientists work as a team. Pathologists look at bodies to figure out the cause of death. Toxicologists test blood and body tissue to look for poisons or chemicals. Forensic engineers reconstruct crime and accident scenes. Fingerprint experts examine print patterns to match them to a **suspect**. Weapons experts study the paths of bullets and special markings left by guns.

LOOKING FOR CLUES

The clues to solve a case are everywhere, if you know where—and how—to look. Forensic scientists are experts at collecting the clues to solve a crime.

Crime-scene investigators must look at all the evidence when trying to solve a case. A witness's memory is not always reliable. **Physical** evidence can give more concrete results, but only if it is **analyzed** properly. Forensic scientists decide which will give them the break they need in order to solve the crime.

SOLVE A CRIME

Let's imagine that a crime has just been committed. A man and a woman have robbed a bank and shot a customer during the raid. How will crime-scene investigators figure out who shot the innocent bystander and made off with a bag full of cash?

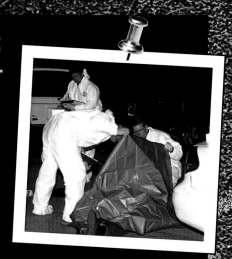

PROTECTING EVIDENCE

The area where the crime took place is blocked off with tape (right). This prevents people from **contaminating** the crime scene. They might add material that would confuse the investigation or damage the evidence left by the criminals.

GET A CLUE

Each bit of evidence is recorded, photographed, and packaged to take back to the lab. This takes patience, special equipment, and a keen eye. Searchers are very careful. Even the smallest fiber might be an important clue.

Before a dead body is moved from the scene, its position is marked on the ground.

WITNESS ACCOUNTS

In our pretend investigation, the bank's janitor told police he saw a woman chewing gum on the front steps before coming into the bank. A teller said she saw the male suspect scrape his knuckle when stuffing cash into his bag, leaving behind a small blood sample on the counter. A passer-by found the demand note lying on the sidewalk nearby. Several customers in the bank heard squealing tires after the suspects fled. Finally, a mailman told police he saw a green sedan race away from the bank, leaving tire marks on the pavement.

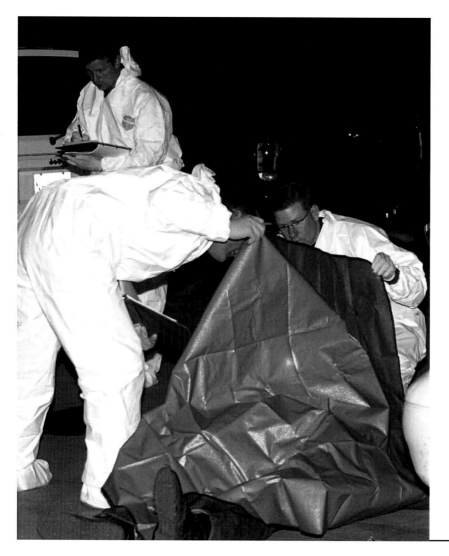

Crime-scene investigators examine a dead body before moving it to the lab for further tests.

Investigators make detailed records of everything they find at a crime scene. Even the smallest detail might be important.

PHYSICAL EVIDENCE

Forensic scientists now have several pieces of evidence: fresh chewing gum from the bank steps, the note used to demand money during the raid, a dead body, and tire marks on the street. A careful search of the area turned up masks in a dumpster nearby, and traces of fibers and hairs left in the bank. There are also blood stains on the counter and several fingerprints left on the bank's glass doors.

> Wasps can be trained to track smells like a dog.

EVERY CONTACT LEAVES A TRACE

Professor Edmond Locard was the director of the first crime lab in Lyon, France, in 1910. He believed that any contact a criminal makes leaves a clue, such as fingerprints or strands of hair. Criminals may also carry fibers or other traces of the crime scene with them as they run away.

SCIENCE SOLUTION

Scientists work by examining a problem to come up with a possible explanation, or **hypothesis**. Then they do experiments to see if their ideas are correct. A crime scene can be treated in the same way. Forensic scientists study the clues and come up with a hypothesis about what happened. Each piece of evidence is tested to see if it fits with the hypothesis. If the test results do not fit, then it is time to come up with another explanation.

TOOLS OF THE TRADE

A crime-scene investigation kit includes:

Fingerprinting kit
Camera
Brushes
Metal mirror
Casting materials (for making copies of footprints)
Magnets (for collecting metal dust)
Tweezers

Scalpel (for cutting and scraping)
Rubber gloves
Sticky labels
Plastic bags
Flashlight
Magnifying glass
Pocket knife
Screwdrivers

An investigator places numbers next to clues. He will then take photos to record where everything was found before taking the evidence back to the lab.

TRAVELING LAB

Every minute counts when trying to solve a crime. By the time a sample is analyzed back at the lab, a suspect could be long gone. Some police departments solve this problem with crime labs in trucks that travel to and work at the scene.

REVEALED

A chemical called luminol produces a blue light when mixed with blood. Luminol spray shows spots of blood that are left behind after someone tries hiding them.

HUNT AND GATHER

Investigators want to record clues left by the criminals and victims, not things introduced to the scene of the crime later on. Investigators wear protective suits, eye goggles, and rubber gloves to keep from contaminating the scene. Flat areas are sprinkled with fine powder. Most of it is then dusted off, but what is left shows any fingerprints. Copies of the prints are recorded on sticky tapes and cards. Other pieces of evidence are photographed before being touched. They are then taken away in plastic bags or containers.

Once the clues have been collected, they must be examined closely by a team of forensice scientists.

Examining evidence helps make sense of the clues. Some of these clues are dead ends. Some clues lead to other evidence and give police hints about where to focus their investigation. By looking at each clue and figuring out how they relate to each other, forensic scientists can help build a picture of what happened.

Every item collected from the crime scene is checked for prints and blood.

SUSPECTS

A green car matching the witness's description is stopped, and its passengers, a man and a woman, are taken in for questioning. There is a gun in the car, but no money is found.

CRIME LAB

The Federal Bureau of Investigations (FBI) has the most **sophisticated** crime lab in North America. Over the years, the FBI has processed millions of pieces of evidence from all over the world.

FIRED UP

Ballistics experts know all about guns. Ballistic fingerprinting is the science of matching bullets with the firearms that shot them.

CE BAG

(Continuity)

SUSPECT ONE

When someone is arrested, his or her fingerprints are always recorded. At our pretend crime scene, one of the fingerprints from the glass doors matched the prints taken from the arrested man. This tells police that the man was at the bank, but it does not tell them when he was there. A **graphologist** shows that the suspect's handwriting matches the words on the demand note. The man must have written it. The **DNA** in the blood left behind by the male robber at the bank also matches the male suspect's. So police now know it was him who was stuffing money into the bag.

Police measure the tire marks made during an accident. This information can be used to identify the vehicles involved and figure out how fast they were traveling before the crash.

Fingerprints show police which people were at the bank, but not when they were there.

EXAMINE THE FACTS

Forensic dentists identify people by their teeth. You can try it yourself. Have three friends take a bite out of an apple. Each one then bites down on a styrofoam plate. Mix up the apples and plates. Use a magnifying glass to try to match the bites in the apples with those in the plates.

The shape of blood spatters tells forensic scientists about the way the bleeding person was injured.

SUSPECT TWO

Lipstick on the gum found outside the bank matches the brand worn by the female suspect. Hair taken from one of the face masks matches the woman's. She must have been at the scene, but there is no evidence she took part in the crime.

DEAD-END CLUES

The robber had put the demand note in his mouth while he stuffed the money in the bag. A forensic dentist tries to match the teeth marks on the note with those of the suspect, but there is no good match. The tire marks from the scene match those of the suspects' green sedan, but that type of tire is very common. The marks outside the bank were not necessarily made by the suspects' car.

LAB TYPES

The FBI crime lab has several divisions: The Questioned Documents Unit checks whether documents are **authentic**. The Trace Evidence Unit identifies trace evidence, such as fibers collected at a crime scene (pictured). The **Latent** Print Operation Unit examines fingerprints. The Paints and Polymers Unit analyzes paints, tapes and glues found at crime scenes. The Firearms and Toolmarks Unit identifies the weapons used in crimes.

15

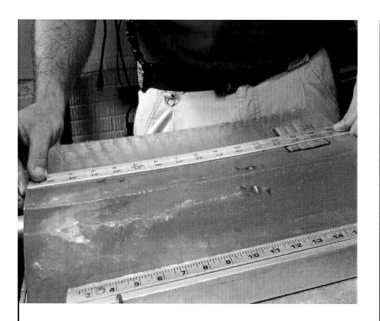

This block of gel has the same hardness as a human body. A forensic scientist has fired a bullet into it. This will help him figure out how powerful a suspect's gun is.

SCRAPING THE BARREL

As a bullet is shot, it spins around against the gun's barrel. This creates marks on the casing of the bullet. Each gun creates a **unique** pattern of markings. The gun recovered from the suspects' car is fired at the ballistics lab. That bullet is compared with the one found inside the body of the murder victim. They are placed side by side under a comparison **microscope**. Both bullets have the same markings. This proves that the gun was used in the murder. But who shot the gun?

TRACKING

Analyzing bits of **debris** from an explosion helps investigators track down the person who built the bomb. In 1996, a bomb exploded in a park in Atlanta, Georgia, while the city was hosting the Olympic Games. A woman was killed, and more than 100 others were injured. Forensic experts (below) collected every piece of the bomb. They noticed that it was similar to others that had gone off in the region. This led them to a suspect—Eric Robert Rudolph. More tests showed that the metal in nails in the Atlanta bomb was identical to other nails stored at Rudolph's home. In 2005, Rudolph was sent to prison for life.

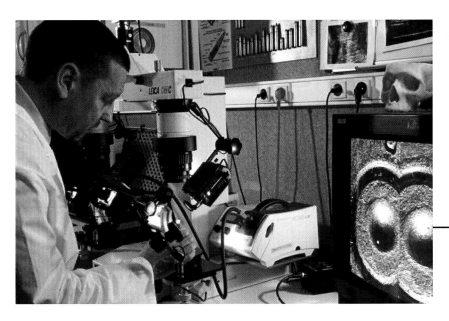

A ballistics expert has two bullets under a microscope. One has been found at a crime scene, and the other comes from a gun fired in a lab test. The patterns made by the gun on the bullets are being compared on the screen.

GUNSHOT RESIDUE

When a gun is fired, a powdery **residue** blasts out of it. The female suspect's skin is covered in this residue. Forensic scientists lift a sample off her fingers using sticky tape. The mix of chemicals in the residue from the gun and collection tape match exactly. This proves that it was the woman suspect who had recently fired the gun.

A gun makes a pattern of markings on every bullet fired from it.

ROBOT DETECTIVES

Making bombs safe is very dangerous. So, why send a person when an armored robot can do the job? An operator guides the robot using hand controls and remote cameras. This way, he or she can stay at a safe distance as the robot investigates the explosive device. The latest robots have X-ray scanners to see inside bombs and sensors that can "smell" the type of explosive used.

IDENTIFICATION

Forensic scientists also work to identify dead bodies and figure out how they died.

Often, the victims of murder have a driver's license or other identification that tells police who they are. But what about victims who do not have any identification? Investigators can check fingerprints against their records. Many people have X-rays of their teeth stored by their dentists. The shape of your teeth is as unique as your fingerprint. Investigators can check the victims' teeth shapes against dental records to identify bodies.

DNA CODE

Each person is made up of millions of cells. These cells contain a chemical code called DNA. Only identical twins share the same DNA code. By decoding the DNA in skin, blood, or hair samples, investigators can use this information to help match the sample with a victim or a criminal. They use the DNA to grow a "genetic fingerprint" on gel. The patterns in each print show which **genes** the DNA contains.

TOOTH AND BONE

Teeth and bones are the most **durable** parts of the human body. This fact comes in handy for forensic investigators. They use tooth patterns to link a criminal to a crime. Bones also can tell a story. If bones are broken or crushed, it can show investigators that violence was used. Was it murder?

041G780008294A

Unidentified bodies are kept in refrigerators inside buildings called morgues.

PRINTS PROCESS

Juan Vucetich, from Argentina in South America, was the first detective to find criminals by their fingerprints in 1892. Ever since then, police have used this method to help link suspects to their crimes. Fingerprint **technology** is getting better every day, with **scanners** replacing ink prints. Plus, police can match fingerprints against millions held on computer **databases** with just a few clicks of a mouse.

People do not just leave fingerprints. Footprints can also identify criminals. Forensic scientists look for unique marks on the soles of shoes.

"Digital fingerprints do not get smudged."

PRINT PATTERNS

No two people have the same fingerprints. Each print has unique patterns of arches, **whorls**, and loops. When the police arrest a suspect, they take his or her fingerprints. A complete sample includes two sets of prints. Rolled **impressions** are made by rolling an inked finger from side to side across the paper. This rolling motion ensures a complete print is made. Plain impressions are made when the fingers are pressed flat onto the fingerprint card at the same time.

Plain impressions are more like the ones found at crime scenes, but they do not show the whole pattern on a fingertip. That is needed to identify a person properly.

LIVE SCAN

Ink is not the only way to take prints. The police also use a scanner to make **digital** images of prints. Scanned fingerprints do not get smudged and can be sent in e-mails to anywhere in the world, where computers can analyze them right away.

Crime-scene investigators make hidden prints show up by brushing dark powder over surfaces.

REAL LIFE

Marc Labranche is a senior fingerprint examiner with the Royal Canadian Mounted Police (RCMP) in Ottawa. His job is to match fingerprints found at crime scenes from across Canada with any of the 3.8 million existing fingerprint records on the RCMP's computer system. The Automated Fingerprint Identification System identifies the unique collection of loops and curves of any fingerprint. The computer automatically highlights the different patterns and uses them to search through the prints of known criminals.

Pathologists examine the skeleton of a person who was murdered in the 1980s.

BODY CLUES

A pathologist is a doctor who conducts autopsies. An autopsy is an operation carried out on a dead body to find out when, why, and how the person died. Pathologists look for bruises, scratches, broken bones, and bites. They also find the paths bullets took through the body and look for foreign substances in the body. They search for samples of the killer's DNA. They may check under the dead person's fingernails for clues.

AFTER DEATH

- Body temperature drops slowly after death. It takes 24 hours to reach the temperature of the surroundings.
- Rigor mortis — meaning "the stiffness of death" — sets in within three hours.
- Eyes develop a thin, cloudy coating within three hours.
- Skin color changes as hours, days, and weeks pass.
- How much food has been digested in the stomach shows when the victim last ate a meal.

TINY DETECTIVES

Diatoms are tiny, single-celled **algae** that live in the ocean and river water. When a body is found in water, scientists look for diatoms to tell them about what happened to the victim. As the body sunk, water flooded into its mouth and lungs. If the person was alive in the water, his or her beating heart would have pumped the diatoms from the lungs into other parts of the body. If the person was already dead when he or she hit the water, diatoms would only make it as far as the lungs.

Diatoms have tiny shells made from silica, a hard substance found in sand. The tough shell means diatoms are not damaged and are easy to find—even inside a dead body.

FORGERY AND FRAUD

From forging signatures to raiding computer hard drives, criminals are finding new and craftier ways to trick people out of their money.

Greedy criminals can use **forgery** to make fake documents like passports so they can pretend to be someone else. They make inexpensive **counterfeits** of dollar bills and other valuable products. And criminals make easy money through **fraud**—they trick people into giving them money and give nothing in return. Computers, scanners, and printers are useful tools for fraudsters—and for investigators, too!

COPIERS

Faking a signature is the most basic forgery. Faked signatures are used to forge checks, create false contracts, or even to make fake autographs of famous people. However, it is not as easy as it looks to copy a signature. Handwriting analysts can spot a fake by comparing writing samples from a suspect with the forgery.

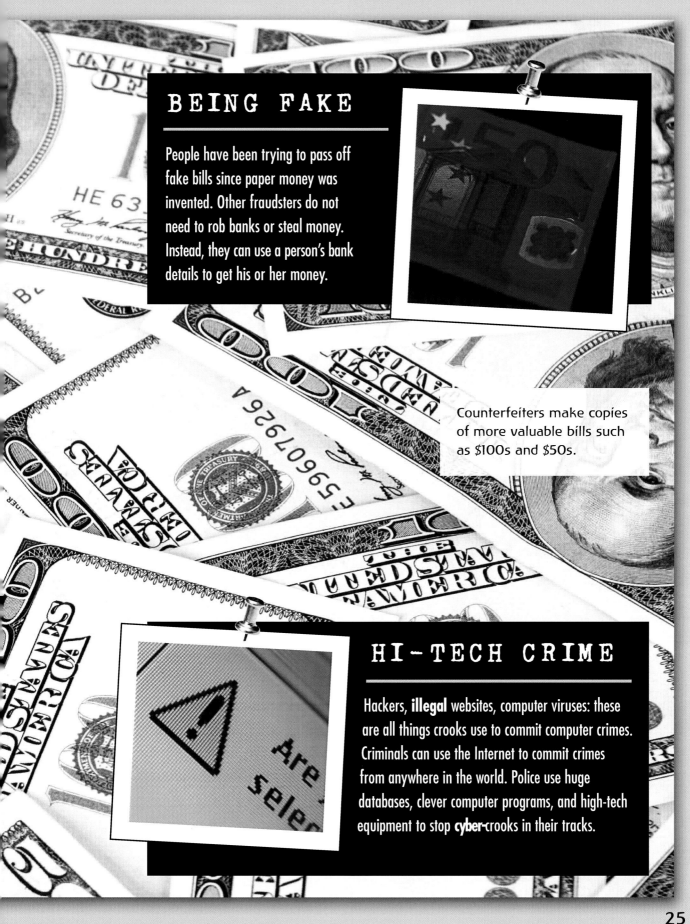

BEING FAKE

People have been trying to pass off fake bills since paper money was invented. Other fraudsters do not need to rob banks or steal money. Instead, they can use a person's bank details to get his or her money.

Counterfeiters make copies of more valuable bills such as $100s and $50s.

HI-TECH CRIME

Hackers, **illegal** websites, computer viruses: these are all things crooks use to commit computer crimes. Criminals can use the Internet to commit crimes from anywhere in the world. Police use huge databases, clever computer programs, and high-tech equipment to stop **cyber-**crooks in their tracks.

HIDDEN SIGNS

Money has several built-in features that make it very difficult to copy. Special printing, known as intaglio (in-tal-yo), presses shapes into the paper. A **hologram** on the bill is hard to forge and is expensive to make. Special inks are used that change color slightly when viewed from different positions.

TO CATCH A KILLER

Each person has a unique way of writing. Writing experts compare the shape of the letters in a suspect's handwriting with writing from a crime scene or forgery. A famous case that used handwriting as evidence was the murder of Charles Lindberg's son in 1932. Lindberg was a world-famous flyer and politician. The writing on ransom notes was matched to documents written by Bruno Richard Hauptmann (below). Hauptmann was executed for the murder in 1936.

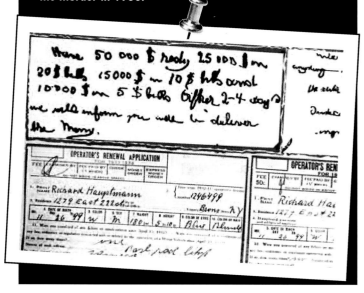

Chromatography is a used to separate ingredients in substances. It can be used to analyze inks on forged documents or counterfeit money. Here's what you'll need for your own ink investigation: A black non-permanent marker pen, an empty glass, a white coffee filter paper, water, and a spoon.

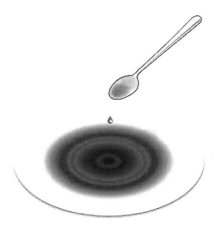

1) Draw a large dot in the center of the coffee filter.
2) Rest the filter on an empty glass or cup.
3) Drip a few drops of water onto the dot so the center of the paper is wet.
5) Leave for a few hours.

Black ink is made up of **pigments**. The water carries different colors along the paper at different speeds. This causes rings of color as the paper dries. An ink can be identified by its set of rings.

The ink in this €50 (euro) bill changes color under **ultraviolet** light. In normal light the pink stars look yellow. Forged notes will not change color like this.

Metal threads are woven through the paper, and show up in bright light. Watermarks—very faint images hidden in the paper—are made by varying the thickness of the bill. You can see a watermark only by holding the bill up to the light.

CLEVER COPIERS

Some photocopiers can recognize dollar bills and will print only blank sheets when someone tries to copy money. Other copiers print an invisible code on paper. The code can be used to track a counterfeit bill back to its source. British bills carry a picture of the country's queen. Her eyes have several tiny rings inside them. These rings create smudge-like patterns when photocopied.

Some photocopiers print an invisible code on paper so forgeries can be tracked to their source.

COMPUTER CRIME

The Internet connects criminals to their victims so they never even have to see each other. Some criminals pretend to be someone else to trick their victims. They may steal a victim's information so they can **access** their bank accounts or credit cards. Criminal computer experts are called hackers. They plant software on their victim's computer.

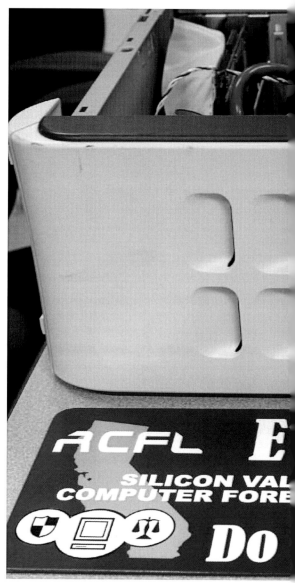

REAL LIFE

On May 4, 2000, the ILOVEYOU virus infected 10 percent of all computers connected to the Internet. Users received an e-mail with the subject header saying ILOVEYOU. If they clicked on the attachment, a program called a worm was sent to everyone in that user's email address book. Over a few days, this powerful virus spread across the world.

Spyware records what a user types and c on when using the computer, so the hacke can figure out their passwords. Programs called bots allow the hacker to control an person's computer so he or she can use it commit crimes. Modern police services ha computer experts who can dig up the evic of crimes stored on people's computers.

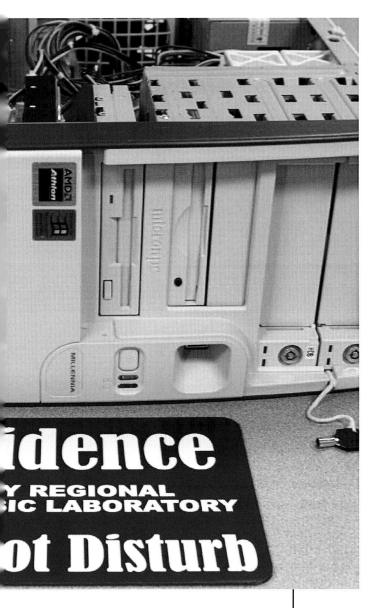

Each computer transaction leaves a record. Investigators follow these clues to trace criminals.

Even when computer files are deleted, parts of them are still stored on the hard drive. Investigators can piece the files back together.

CYBER-SLEUTHS

It is difficult for police to stop cyber-criminals because they might work in many different countries. However, each computer **transaction** leaves a record. Investigators follow these clues to trace the crooks.

Computer databases store information about crimes. Programs are used to search through this **data** to find clues.

GLOSSARY

access The ability to use something

algae Tiny living things that make food from sunlight in the same way as plants

analyzed Studied in a scientific way

authentic When something is real and not an imitation

ballistics The study of how objects, including bullets, travel through the air

casting Copying the exact shape of an object using a mold

chromatography A way of separating a substance into its ingredients

contaminating Adding unwanted substances

counterfeits Fake versions of something, usually paper money

cyber To do with computers

data Information stored on a computer

databases Collections of information stored on a computer

debris The broken remains left by a violent event

digital Recorded with a code of numbers, or digits, on a computer

DNA Short for deoxyribonucleic acid, the chemical that carries a person's code for life

durable Very hard wearing so something does not rub away or break up easily

entomologist An expert on insects

experiments Tests that show whether an idea is correct or incorrect

evidence A clue that shows what has happened during a crime

fibers Thin threads, for example from clothes

forgery Something that has been copied or altered by a criminal

fraud To get money or other valuables by tricking people into giving it to you

genes The coded instructions used by the body to grow and work properly

graphologist An expert on handwriting

habitats Places where plants or animals lives

hologram A picture that changes shape when you look at it from a different direction

hypothesis An idea that might explain a mystery

illegal Against the law

impressions Images made when something is pressed onto paper

investigators People who look for clues and figure out what happened at a crime scene

latent Hidden from view

microscope A machine for looking at tiny objects.

odor A smell

physical Made of something that can be measured

pigments Colored substances used in paints and dyes

portable Something that is designed to be carried

residue A small amount of liquid or powder left behind on a surface or in a container

scanner A machine that turns pictures into computer files

sophisticated Very advanced and good at doing something

suspect A person who is being investigated for carrying out a crime

technology When science is used to make something useful

transaction When two people or computers exchange something, such as money or information

ultraviolet Invisible light that makes certain substances glow in the dark

unique Being the only one

whorls A rounded, spiral-shaped pattern

FURTHER INFORMATION

Books

Crime & Detection by Brian Lane. New York, NY: DK Publishing, 2005.

Crime Scene Investigation by Paul Mauro. New York, NY: Scholastic, 2003.

Forensic Science by Ron Fridell. Minneapolis, MN: Lerner Publications Co., 2007.

Forensics: Solving the Crime by Tabatha Yeatts. Minneapolis, MN: Oliver Press, 2001.

Solving Crimes: Pioneers of Forensic Science by Ron Fridell. New York, NY: Franklin Watts, 2000.

Websites

Chromatography Science Fair:
http://www.itsjustabox.com/Sciencefair.htm

Crimeline: The History pf Forensic Science:
http://www.crimezzz.net/forensic_history/index.htm

Federal Bureau of Investigation Kids' Page:
http://www.fbi.gov/fbikids.htm

Internet Super Heros:
http://www.internetsuperheros.org/

National Library of Medicine: Forensic Views of the Body:
http://www.nlm.nih.gov/visibleproofs/galleries/cases/index.html

INDEX